Nordic and Baltic Security in the 1990s

Richard Latter

June 1992

WILTON PARK PAPER 56

Report based on Wilton Park Conference 382: 1–5 June 1992. Reshaping Nordic and Baltic Security: How to Maintain Stability and Develop Co-operation in Northern Europe?

LONDON: HMSO

First published 1992

ISBN 0 11 701708 6
ISSN 0953–8542

Contents

1 Introduction

The major changes in the European security system, deriving principally from the collapse of the Soviet Union but also increasingly influenced by the evolution of the European Community towards deeper European union, have altered radically the security concerns of Baltic and Nordic states. While military concerns remain, not least the presence of former Soviet military units in the Baltic states, Poland and eastern Germany, it is the economic dimension of the region's security which is increasingly to the fore. The task of building successful market economies in the former WTO states of the region is immense and requires genuine co-operation between the old adversaries of the Cold War; failure to build economic stability in these countries will result in social and political unrest which will inevitably spill over into inter-state relations in the region. The worsening economic situations in Poland, the Baltic states and Russia are not encouraging, and the 'Old West' has yet fully to grasp the fact that its own security interests require a level of commitment to, and involvement in, reconstruction in the 'Old East', which it has thus far been unwilling to contemplate.

However, the economic woes within the region should not divert attention from the genuine military problems which remain. While the national military establishments evolving in the countries of the former Soviet Union have been severely weakened by its demise, there is every reason to believe that Russia will remain a major European military power, one which will retain significant military assets within, or adjacent to, the Nordic and Baltic regions. Russian or CIS strategic nuclear forces will continue to operate in the High Arctic and from the Kola Peninsula. Even before the collapse of the Soviet Union it was noted that "the risk of an armed conflict in the High North has clearly decreased. A realistic analysis can, however, only include an elucidation of a geo-strategic condition and the available military capacity. Good intentions can change for the worse rapidly."[1]

---

[1] Tauno Nieminen, "Flank or Front, An Assement of Military-political Developments in the High North", *Finnish Defence Studies*, No. 2, War College, Helsinki, 1991, p. 37.

The risk of war between the United States and Russia has undoubtedly been further reduced, yet Russian military capabilities *will* remain and the uncertainties of Russian political and economic life are such that stability in its internal and foreign relations cannot be guaranteed. Whatever the future, however, "the Arctic Ocean can be expected to gain in strategic importance in the future and to become an increasingly focal area for military operations. Under-ice operations will increase as the enabling technologies are developed. The air space of the Arctic will continue to be important for the purposes of early warning and as a route for strategic air assets".[2] Any reshaping of Nordic and Baltic security must take due account of these factors.

Of more short-term concern in the military field is the presence of former Soviet military forces in the Baltic states, eastern Germany and Poland. While the withdrawal from Germany appears to be moving smoothly towards completion in 1994, and an almost total withdrawal from Poland has been agreed for the end of 1992, serious differences exist in the Baltic states between the new governments, the Russian regime and the former Soviet Union's (FSU) military commanders in the region itself. While withdrawal has been agreed in principle, tensions are likely to remain high until an agreed timetable for withdrawal has been established. Unfortunately the issue appears to be of low priority for the Russian authorities, who also stress the need for adequate rehousing of troops returning to their homeland. More disturbingly, the linkage of the troops' presence with the existence of Russian minorities in the Baltic states may have more sinister implications. The apparent unwillingness of some elements of the Soviet military to withdraw under 'any circumstances' is linked with the broader problem of military-civilian relations within Russia: whether conservative elements in the military may yet thwart the movement towards democracy and economic liberalisation, possibly through a successful coup. The future evolution of a stable military situation in the area remains largely dependent upon events in the former Soviet Union.

---

[2] Ibid, p. 40.

These military issues, however, are currently outweighed by the serious economic problems which confront the region, as the Baltic states, Russia, Poland and eastern Germany seek to establish viable economies: "the most dangerous and urgent problem for the Baltic countries for the moment is probably the desperate economic situation: the trade links to the East are to a great extent cut off. New links to the West have not yet been established. There is no hard currency available for vital imports of for instance energy, medicine or fodder grain".[3] Establishing viable economies and currencies, replacing command economic systems by market systems and developing sound trade links in the region and beyond are all immediate priorities. To meet these needs bilateral relations are being established, with the Nordic countries and Germany taking the lead in investing in the East, and multilateral contacts have been established via the IMF and World Bank.

All recognise that the European Community will be a key player in this process of reconstruction and development; Association Agreements are already in place for Poland, Hungary and Czechoslovakia, but it is clear that yet more aid and assistance will be required from the West. In the Baltic region itself realignment of relationships with the European Community is occurring; the Swedish and Finnish applications for membership will affect fundamentally the political relationship between the Baltic region and its southern neighbours. This combination of anticipated increasing EC involvement and the need for economic reconstruction is not peculiar to the Baltic; being common to central and south eastern Europe and the new states of the former Soviet Union. However, in the Baltic region there is a unique aspect to this 'cocktail' of problems; the existence of a Nordic tradition.

Some argue that Nordic identity is in crisis:[4] "In security terms,

---

[3] Mr Uffe Ellemann-Jensen, Minister of Foreign Affairs of Denmark, in the London Chamber of Commerce and Industry, Chatham House, January 24, 1992, Keynote address at the conference *the Re-integration of the Baltic States into the World Community.*

[4] Ole Wæver, "Nordic Nostalgia: Northern Europe After the Cold War", *International Affairs*, 68: 1 (1992), pp. 77–102.

Nordic identity was defined by having lower military tensions than Central Europe. In socio-economic terms, Nordic identity was dependent on the competition between capitalism and communism, offering a third way. At a deeper level, Norden represented a model of the enlightened, anti-militaristic society that was superior to the old Europe".[5] Ole Wæver notes that "these identities have disintegrated. The confrontation in Central Europe has disappeared; the competition between capitalism and communism is over. Now the key dynamics in European events are the two processes of 1989 and of 1992; the key concepts are political freedom rights, the free market and integration. Suddenly the sources of the future are to be found not in Norden, but on the Continent. The less-European identity of 'Norden' is no longer a promise, but a threat – the threat of being periphery".[6]

The adjustment of Nordic policies to this new situation will certainly influence the evolution of the Baltic security subsystem. Possible options for the Nordic states appear to include: abandoning the traditional 'Nordic' approach, alternatively reinvigorating Nordic co-operation, "possibly in new forms and mainly in relation to, perhaps as a sub-group inside, the European Community",[7] or adopting a third way by attempting to launch co-operation in the Baltic region "as a replacement for, a reformulation of, Nordic co-operation".[8] This last option appears to be receiving increased attention. For example, Danish Minister of Foreign Affairs Elleman-Jensen said "the Baltic Sea is no longer a blind alley on the outskirts of Europe, but will once more become a centre of activity and prosperity, become what some people refer to as the *Baltic Growth Zone*. ... Indeed I see this area as one of four or five main areas of development in Europe. I share the conviction that within the coming ten years or so, the map of Europe will be dominated by one very big economic power centre located around the Rhine, supplemented by four supporting regional centres. One of these centres is the region around the

---

[5] *Ibid*, p. 77.
[6] *Ibid*.
[7] *Ibid*, p. 78.
[8] *Ibid*.

Baltic Sea".[9] The exact form that such Baltic co-operation will take and its relationship with the European Community have yet to be established.

The relationship established between a possible future Baltic co-operative entity and the European Community will affect directly national security problems and the broader evolution of stable security relations in the Baltic and Nordic regions. For example, the European Community has already emphasised conditionality of aid and trade links upon respect for human and minority rights; in the short term, it may be better placed than a nascent Baltic entity to promote a peaceful resolution of ethnic problems. This problem is particularly acute in the Baltic republics, not least in Latvia, where only 52 per cent of the total population are Latvian, because of inward migration of Russians during the Soviet period.[10]

At a broader level, the Baltic/EC relationship would crucially affect decisions on the region's collective security/defence arrangements. While much stress has been laid on the CSCE process in the Nordic countries, the enthusiam for some form of CSCE collective security arrangement appears to be waning. The difficulties of such a situation where "none would be designated as enemy, each would assume the role of peace-keeper, and all (minus one) would be ready to move against the aggressor in their midst when so authorized by the collective"[11] appears to be unworkable, not least because the idea "that the many will assemble overwhelming power against the one to defeat the culprit"[12] simply does not hold up in a nuclear world. How then should the states of the Baltic organise their security?

Norway, Denmark and Germany continue to rely on the collective

---

[9] Uffe Ellemann-Jensen, speech in the London Chamber of Commerce and Industry, Chatham House, January 24, 1992.
[10] Juris Dreifelds, "Immigration and Ethnicity in Latvia", *Journal of Soviet Nationalities,* Winter 1990–92, Volume 1, No. 4, pp. 43–81.
[11] Josef Joffe, "Collective Security and the Future of Europe: Failed Dreams and Dead Ends", *Survival,* Spring 1992, p. 37.
[12] *Ibid,* p. 45.

defence arrangement provided by NATO, but the Germans at least appear to support the evolution of a genuine European Community security policy and the formation of the Franco-German corps offers the prospect of an exclusively EC-based defence capability. It is unclear how far traditionally neutral Sweden and Finland will be prepared to co-operate in such an evolution of EC policy when they secure membership, and in the near term NATO and NACC are more attractive to the Poles, the Balts and indeed the Russians and Ukrainians. Yet, membership of the Alliance is not on offer, at least in the short term, and the problems of developing a stable security relationship with Russia remain. Can it be that the concept of neutrality, until recently 'written off' as a relic from the Cold War, may yet prove useful?

Neutrality may yet be attractive in the current period of transition. Many of the countries in the region already meet the core conditions: they are not members of any alliance; they are committed to avoidance of involvement in any war; and they either have no foreign bases, or are seeking their removal. But for the Balts and the Poles the problem of Russia remains and links with the West are a priority in countries where 'Cold War' attitudes towards the Russian neighbour persist. Also many doubt that armed neutrality represents a serious option, given the high costs involved and the poor state of local economies. Yet much depends on Western attitudes, and these remain ambivalent. "Are Western governments committed to the incorporation of Central Europe in the Western economic and security systems, or are they seeking merely to ensure that the region remains stable outside the West European political sub-system? . . . Western policies are geared at least to achieving stability, and this must mean that they favour at least a close association of the Central European states with the West European system".[13] However, this does not preclude neutrality; Sweden and Finland, while neutral, have been very much part of the 'Western' system.

For countries in the region, which are not members of NATO or an

---

[13] Richard Latter, 'NATO and Neutrality in Europe', in *Jane's NATO Handbook, 1991–92,* Bruce George (ed), p. 407.

EC-based defence arrangement and fail to secure or opt to reject such membership, some form of *de facto* neutrality may be an inevitable consequence. Existing members of the Alliance and of the EC, as well as the states themselves, need to consider whether this is a situation which would enhance European stability. The form of 'neutrality' to be adopted need not necessarily be benign and militarisation of relations cannot be precluded. For example Lithuanian officials appear to have moved from the view that "We are a small state and for this reason we cannot use the defence strategy and weapons philosophy of large states. In our opinion the total defence system used in Scandinavia would also fit the needs of Lithuania",[14] to a rather different reference point: "We are very interested in the Israeli defence system. The pressures on Israel are similar to the pressures on Lithuania".[15] The attractiveness of neutrality will be influenced heavily by the unfolding military situation in the region and by the role which the remaining European alliance, NATO, will play in the decade ahead.

2 Declining Military Risks

The risk of a major European war between Western Europe, the US and Russia has virtually disappeared. There is greater interest in developing some form of pan-European, co-operative security arrangement which would include the West, Russia, Central European states and a considerable number of the former Soviet republics. The on-going debate about inter-locking institutions is predicated on the assumption that some new European security system can be established to minimise the possibility of armed conflict in the region through a combination of crisis management and confidence-building measures. However, this is slow to develop and wars are already occurring in Europe, noticeably in

---

[14] Audrius Butkevicius, Minister of Defence of Lithuania, Vilnius. 'Lithuanian Security: the Military Dimension', p. 9, North Atlantic Assembly Seminar on the Baltic States Security Requirements, 17 December 1991.
[15] Audrius Butkevicius in The JDW Interview, Tony Banks, *Jane's Defence Weekly,* 30 May 1992, p. 952.

Croatia and Bosnia-Herzegovina, while frictions in the FSU are such that armed conflict beyond Nagorno-Karabakh cannot be precluded. Thus, military problems remain for Europeans, including those living in the Baltic region.

The end of the Cold War has exacerbated problems in the area at least for the short-term. The redeployment of large numbers of troops and much equipment from the former European central front to northern Russia, notably the Kaliningrad region and the Kola Peninsula, has resulted in a significant build-up of military force in the Nordic and Baltic areas. In addition, the independence of the Baltic states is generating a high level of friction between former Soviet military forces and these newly 'Nordic' countries. This may yet lead to a more general increase in tension in the region. Furthermore, the relaxation of Western concerns about Russian military power, and the associated reductions in Western defence capabilities, may give rise to situations where Nordic and Baltic countries will have to meet any regional military crisis with reduced support from 'traditional' allies to the south and across the Atlantic.

These factors have undoubtedly contributed to Swedish and Finnish decisions to modernise and improve the capabilities of their respective military establishments; the Finnish Government's decision to purchase F-18 aircraft represents a substantial commitment in this context. Norwegian and Danish commitments to NATO remain undiluted; their recent differences regarding the allocation of the Baltic Sea to NATO's North-Western or Central regions is illustrative of their continued interest. Continued concern about Russian capabilities, if not short-term intentions, is even more intense in the Baltic Republics and Poland, which are, respectively, seeking to establish their own national defence forces and redeploying a significant proportion of their troops and equipment from western to eastern borders.

The continued existence of regional military concerns is paralleled, some analysts argue, by the persistent but broader strategic factors which derive from the Cold War period. Thus, the far

North remains the centre of operations of the Russian nuclear submarine fleet and it retains a large defensive military presence in the Kola Peninsula to protect its strategic assets, which includes a capability for military landings in northern Norway. In addition, the Baltic, Norwegian and Northern Seas form a buffer zone for the West should American reinforcement of Europe prove necessary. Outer protection of the Russian heartland remains a priority for the Russian military in the North, although this task has been made more difficult in the Baltic, given Russian withdrawal from East Germany and Poland and the Baltic States' independence.

These military factors and capabilities remain unchanged despite the positive evolution of East-West relations. Their future importance to the West will be linked with the overall strategic situation between East and West; successful implementation of START and subsequent nuclear arms reduction agreements, of the CFE Treaty and continued general co-operation will accelerate their already declining relevance. But this positive evolution is itself dependent upon future developments in the unstable former Soviet Union and the long-term progress made in building a European security structure. The respective roles to be played by the CSCE, the European Community and not least NATO, will affect fundamentally the security of the Baltic littoral states.

The Role of NATO

NATO has adapted to the new international environment: for example, by developing a new strategy, by reducing its military forces and re-organising what remains (eg by developing rapid reaction forces), by developing multinational units, and by a new emphasis on dialogue with its former opponents via the North Atlantic Co-operation Council (NACC). While the Alliance retains its integrated military structure and has been careful to retain an effective military capability, it has recognised that the single major threat posed by the Soviet Union has disappeared, and that a new emphasis on its political role and on building co-operation and confidence with its former adversaries is required.

All agree that NATO remains an insurance policy and a force for stability during a period of change in the European political and security system, not least because it ensures a continued US link. However, it remains an open question whether the Alliance will continue as a collective *defence* organisation, perhaps with an expanded membership, or fulfil a wider brief by organising collective *security* arrangements for the continent.

Adopting this wider brief is rejected by those who believe that the Alliance will be weakened to such a degree that it will be unable to fulfil its past collective defence role. Others point to the inevitability of a conflict with other institutions, for example, the CSCE. It remains an open question whether European security affairs will be dominated by a WEU-EC-CSCE combination, or by the NATO-NACC-CSCE alternative, or indeed whether a complex combination of interlocking institutions involving all of these organisations will develop.[16] The current relative weakness of the possible alternatives to NATO is recognised as they lack adequate financial and staff resources; thus, in the near term (for the next five years) NATO is likely to remain the key security instrument for West European states.

What are the implications of this debate for the Nordic and Baltic states? In fact the short-term effects are likely to be minimal. Only the extension of NATO membership would fundamentally alter the region's security balance and this is unlikely given divisions within the Alliance over the wisdom of such an approach. The evolution of a co-ordinated EC security and defence policy seems unlikely to progress far before 1996 when WEU may come to the fore as the EC 'security unit'; current problems over the ratification of the Maastricht Treaty have, however, called even this into doubt. Similarly the evolution of the CSCE into a genuinely pan-European security entity lies far in the future. Thus, the military aspects of Baltic states' security policies seem likely to continue much as before, with Denmark, Germany and Norway remaining

---

[16] For a more detailed coverage of European Security Structures see: 'Defence in Transition', David Bolton, in *Royal United Services Institute and Brassey's Defence Yearbook,* 1992, pp. 3–18.

in NATO, and Sweden and Finland retaining independent defence capabilities. Fundamental changes will occur only in the East where security policies are in flux following the break-up of the Soviet empire. The future evolution of Russian, Polish and Baltic Republic policies provides the real dynamic for change in the Baltic area; their policies will affect developments in their Western neighbours more fundamentally than any debate about the 'alphabet soup' of Western-dominated institutions!

3 Russian Instability and Sensitivity

The evolution of Baltic and Nordic security will be more strongly affected by the Russian Government's response to the myriad of problems it faces nationally, rather than those which are peculiar to the Baltic region itself. The latter tend to be of low priority to a government faced with political instability, severe economic dislocation, associated social problems, and numerous international problems deriving from the break-up of the Soviet Union.

Future Russian policy in the Baltic will be affected by the outcome of the political struggle taking place between conservatives and radicals in Moscow; whether there will be a successful evolution of democracy or a return to more autocratic forms of government, backed by a resurgent *nomenklatura,* is a key factor. However, some trends are likely to continue whatever the outcome: the creation of a Russian army of reduced size, perhaps 1,200,000 men, seems certain. The development of a Russian strategic doctrine is already well-advanced; it will probably include, for example: a commitment to maintain the external borders of Russia, rejection of first use of weapons of mass destruction, plans to meet potential threats which might lead to the domination of Russia by regional neighbours or globally, the commitment to defend the human rights of Russians outside Russia, a reiteration of the need for co-operation via the CIS, the CSCE and other European institutions, to build stability and to prevent war.

The Russian Government's ability to carry forward such a doctrine and to establish democracy securely is dependent upon a successful resolution of the country's economic problems. The break-up of the Soviet Union has severely dislocated the Russian economy and industrial production. Falls in output threaten democracy and the breaking of industrial ties between the former Soviet republics is severely damaging Russian output. Other problems include: the unclear status of the Rouble, resulting partly from the plans of the newly independent republics to establish their own currencies, a huge Rouble overhang which is generating inflation, and the general break-down in the distribution of raw materials, spare parts, currency to pay wages, etc. All of these problems have been exacerbated by Russia's new foreign policy; the ending of COMECON and the decision to conduct trade with near neighbours only in hard currency has dislocated severely Russian trade with its neighbours. Commitments to support arms embargoes against, for example, Iraq and Libya, have reduced Russian earnings from arms exports.

The response of the Russian Government has been to opt for a liberalisation of prices and a privatisation programme, linked with efforts to decentralise the economy and to reduce corruption. The aims are to halt the decline in economic output and to establish an attractive environment for foreign investment.

The role which the West should play in rebuilding the Russian economy is controversial. While some argue the need for a massive infusion of Western finance, many caution that the Russian economy is unable to make use effectively of such assistance and that it will be wasted. Although limited amounts of government aid and humanitarian assistance are helpful and welcome, it is access to the international financial institutions such as the IMF and World Bank, with associated restrictions on economic policy, and foreign private direct investment which may bring genuine progress. Such investment appears likely to be concentrated in certain sectors initially, for example, in high-tech industry, agriculture, transport, construction and raw materials, notably oil, gas and gold. Success here would enable Russia to earn considerable amounts of hard currency with which to finance further development.[17]

Although Russian problems in the Baltic region pale into insignificance in comparison with their other problems, one 'local' issue may yet affect fundamentally Russia's chances for overall success in developing democracy and a market economy: how to organise the withdrawal of Russian troops from the Baltic Republics.

While withdrawal has been agreed in principle, subsequent negotiations have failed to establish a timetable, much less an end point for the withdrawal process. Key issues for the Russians include: re-housing the officers withdrawn, payment for installations left in the Baltic states and for the costs of maintaining 'garrisons' in the region since their 'liberation' from German occupation in 1940, and the ownership of weapons systems located in the region. The chronic unemployment in Russia exacerbates problems of re-location. In addition, the existence of substantial Russian minorities in the Baltic states has resulted in organised campaigns for the troops to remain for their protection. The Russian Government faces a dilemma, caught between the vociferous demands of the new Baltic Governments for early troop withdrawal and the possibility that orders for such a withdrawal may be refused by local military commanders; what would amount to a break-down of civilian control over the Russian military could provide the flash-point for more widespread rebellion and thus threaten to undermine the whole democratisation process. It is therefore unsurprising that the Russian Government has failed actively to promote withdrawal of the troops.

Related problems for the Russian Government include the redeployment of air defence assets in the Baltic Republics and more importantly, from the Russian military's point of view, the gap in the country's air defence system which would result from

[17] For a more detailed study of Russian economic developments see 'Renovating the Economy of the FSU: A Plan for Action', Morgan Stanley, London, March 1992.

the dismantling of installations or their removal into Russia. In this context the Kaliningrad region remains an important focus for Soviet military activity, serving as a redeployment centre for troops leaving Poland and eastern Germany. In addition, its value as a naval base has increased with the loss of access to naval facilities in the independent Baltic states and Poland; the Russian intention to remain in Kaliningrad, despite the disquiet this causes to its Baltic neighbours, is also backed by vague intentions to develop the area as a free trade port, or economic development zone, playing a key role in future Russian economic reconstruction.

The reaction of 'Western' Baltic and Nordic states to the Russian situation is built upon the twin approaches of: a) maintaining a viable military deterrent in case of negative events in Russia, and b) engaging in constructive dialogue, bilaterally and through multinational institutions such as the NACC and the CSCE. At a more practical level, German and Danish programmes to finance the re-housing of Russian troops, the provision of humanitarian and economic assistance, and the beginnings of small-scale direct investment reinforce Western commitment to supporting the democratisation process. However, these options are difficult for the 'Eastern' Baltic countries, Poland and the Baltic Republics, which lack effective deterrence capability and are themselves in deep economic distress. Their efforts to build security in the Baltic region therefore follow a somewhat different approach.

Poland's Reponse

Poland's priorities after the collapse of the Soviet Union have been to ensure a complete withdrawal of former Soviet troops from its territory, to establish a democratic political system, and to introduce a market economy. These changes have been paralleled by a reorientation of foreign policy towards the West by establishing institutional links through the NACC, the CSCE, and an Association Agreement with the European Community. While the country is *de facto* non-aligned its clear long-term preference is to be tied into a Western collective defence arrangement, probably NATO, while co-operating in the construction of a broader

European system which may develop through the CSCE process. These goals reflect Polish concern about possible Russian revanchism; they seek a collective defence arrangement offering the advantages of membership in a stable defence entity, protection against possible external threats, and preventing any re-nationalisation of Polish defence policy. These advantages are balanced against a possible negative Russian reaction by continued emphasis on developing European collective security arrangements which would include the republics of the former Soviet Union.

Alternative Polish options include the evolution of a confederation from the Baltic to the Black Sea, possibly following initiatives by the Ukraine: "Oleksandr Honcarenko has . . . already advocated co-operation between Ukraine, Belorussia, Moldavia and the East European states on security policy. He specifically excluded Russia from any such security arrangement, arguing that Russia was an Asian, not European, power. It is not surprising that such thinking is present among Ukrainian foreign policy specialists, and it is also likely that similar thinking will be found in Ukrainian Government circles. The principal underlying objective is the containment of Russia. . . . The Ukraine is quite likely to build closer co-operative ties with other East European powers as a counter to Russia. It has been commented previously that the former Warsaw Pact states, particularly Poland and Hungary, encouraged Ukrainian efforts towards independence as they saw it as a barrier against Russian power."[18]

This is a road which the Polish Government may yet follow should its overtures to the West be unsuccessful. In the near term, however, initiatives, for example, by the Visigrad Three, have failed to deal with security matters. The adoption of a neutrality policy, either alone or in an East European confederation, also appears to be unlikely, given the high military spending which would be involved and the dubious efficacy of such a policy in the

---

[18] Mark Smith, 'The Eastern Giants: Russia, Ukraine and European Security', *Whitehall Paper Series,* Royal United Services Institute for Defence Studies, p. 56.

event of a war occurring in Central Europe. Neutrality is only a viable option when it is felt to be better than the possible alternatives and the opportunities offered by possible links with NATO, the NACC, the CSCE and, not least, the European Community, have many attractions.

Poland's links with the European Community are the priority in the short-term, given the lack of immediate Russian threat to the East. In the current vacuum, Polish attention is focused inward, on building democracy and establishing a market economy in order to be able effectively to assert national independence. Poland's 'big bang' shift to the market economy system is fraught with problems which have been complicated by the political instability following inconclusive elections in 1992 and subsequent wrangles between President Walesa and the Polish Sejm. The short-term economic outlook is poor. High inflation rates and growing unemployment are occurring as production levels and investment fall. There is increased disillusionment in the population who have made sacrifices in the belief that their standard of living would rise, and this has failed to occur. State enterprises have been passive and failed to link wages to productivity; given their central role in the Polish economy they act as a break on innovation and change. Only 50 per cent of Western assistance offered ($6 billion by the G24 Group) has been used, mainly because of a lack of expertise and suitable projects in Poland itself.

This dismal picture is offset to some degree by evidence of a flourishing grey/black economy, by the Association Agreement with the European Community guaranteeing market access, and by Western creditor nations forgiving half the country's $40 billion foreign debt. German-Polish joint ventures appear to be flourishing. The key issue remains how best to establish a positive economic situation which reduces the risk of widespread social unrest leading to repression and a possible re-introduction of authoritarian rule.

Thus, at a time when the Russian decision-making élite is looking inward, Polish policy-makers are also focusing primarily on their internal economic and political woes. They recognise the existence of possible future problems with their Eastern neighbour but appear to take the view that these will best be dealt with by building a strong politically and economically vibrant country closely linked to the West European security system. Notwithstanding redeployment of Polish troops to the Eastern border, the possibility of conflict with Russia appears to be low and accepted as such. The contrast between a fairly relaxed Polish attitude and the position taken by the newly independent Baltic Republic Governments is striking.

4 The Baltic States – A Flash Point?

The Baltic States have historically been a battle-ground in which German and Russian rivalries have been contested. This fact, and the Russian domination of the countries since 1940, determine the current security policies of the Estonian, Latvian and Lithuanian Governments. They look to the example of Finland during the Second World War, which successfully resisted Russian military intervention and was able to retain its political and economic independence to the post-War world. The policies of all three states are geared to resist any future military intervention by establishing conventional defence forces.

Thus, while the three countries are by no means identical they have adopted common, but not necessarily co-ordinated, positions on security issues. Priorities include: the development of an effective defence doctrine; establishing sufficient military capability (regular armies, rapid reaction forces, and home guards to act in a support role) to resist intervention and organising infrastructure and personnel to ensure effective border control. All are seeking to negotiate with Russia on troop withdrawals but are organising confrontations between local forces and Russian troops remaining in the region. There is a danger that such confrontations could escalate into military action, although this may not be widespread given the relative weakness of the Baltic forces and the need for the Russians to behave 'responsibly' if they are to retain their positive contacts with the West. Nevertheless, even limited armed conflict would have disastrous political consequences.

The key short-term problem for the Baltic Republic Governments is the removal of the Russian army from their territories: all three countries appealed recently, via the Baltic Assembly, for immediate withdrawal: "Despite the many requests by the Republic of Lithuania, the Republic of Estonia, and the Republic of Latvia, the Baltic Assembly and the Council of the Baltic States, for the unconditional and immediate withdrawal of the Russian army from the Baltic states, the withdrawal has essentially not begun. In addition, by not obeying Baltic state laws or Government resolutions, their sovereignty is still being violated since new Russian soldiers and officers are being brought in. Russia is refusing to hand over state border protection to Lithuania, Estonia and Latvia. This creates the impression that Russia is interested in keeping its army in the Baltic states for a long duration. This poses a danger to the security of the people, hinders the Baltic states from implementing a successful economy and social reforms, from developing democracy and from fortifying independence. The furnace of tension by the Baltic may become an additional factor for instability in Europe".[19] The appeal goes on to state that "The Baltic Assembly considers it is expedient for the CSCE representatives to participate, as authoritative observers, in bilateral negotiations, between Russia and the Baltic states regarding the withdrawal of the Russian army."[20]

All three Baltic states are thus seeking to internationalise the problem through the CSCE process to press for Russian withdrawal. This policy is widely supported in the Baltic states. For example, in a recent Lithuanian referendum on an immediate withdrawal of remaining Russian troops, "90.76 per cent voted in favour while . . . 7.29 per cent voted against. Besides calling for a

---

[19] Appeal by the Baltic Assembly About the Withdrawal of the Russian Army from the Territories of the Baltic States, 31 May, 1992, Palanga.
[20] *Ibid.*

troop withdrawal, the referendum demanded that Moscow pay compensation for the occupation, which began in 1940."[21] The issues of who should pay for the Soviet 'occupation', which military assets belong to Russia and which to the Baltic Republics, accusations of asset-stripping, of smuggling and Russian evasion of local taxation all complicate and increase frictions with the Russian military.

The resulting tensions are exacerbated by the presence of significant Russian-speaking minorities, particularly in Estonia and in Latvia. While these Russians have generally supported the Baltic States' independence, active minorities have been opposed or accused the non-Russian majorities of persecution or discrimination; for example, the conditions to be applied to secure Estonian nationality are controversial and deemed by many Russians to represent a violation of their human rights: deprivation of the right to vote, to participate in privatisation programmes, and fears of expulsion from the Baltic States are particular Russian concerns. On the other hand, the new Governments point to the policy of Russification undertaken since the Second World War and note that the national identity of the local peoples must be preserved.

The West has a key role to play on the human rights issue and must seek to temper local nationalist feeling, if necessary by pointing out that Western economic support and membership of Western institutions is dependent upon proper respect for human rights and proper treatment of minorities. Similarly, Western states can use their good offices to promote a settlement of the troops issue, and seek to ensure that this takes place in an orderly manner, perhaps along the lines agreed for eastern Germany. It is important that the case be made to the Russian Government that their domestic problems are not an acceptable excuse for troops remaining in the Baltic Republics.

It is unclear which 'Western' countries or institutions will take the

---

[1] '90 per cent in Lithuania Insist Russians Go', *International Herald Tribune,* Tuesday, 16 June, 1992.

initiative on these issues; their pursuit through the CSCE process and perhaps via the NACC offer some opportunities for progress. Alternatively, a country or a group of countries may be persuaded to act as a broker between the two sides, with Germany or Sweden, for example, fulfilling this role. However, there seems little prospect that the West will offer security guarantees of a concrete nature to the Baltic states; in the absence of a NATO commitment it is unlikely that the Nordic states or Germany acting alone would take on this role. The overall consensus appears to be that negotiations should be conducted via the CSCE process and bilaterally between the Baltic states and the Russian Government.

What is needed is a movement away from the current atmosphere of confrontation towards one of genuine co-operation; for example, the future of Kaliningrad should be discussed less in terms of ownership, of possible re-drawing of borders (a key to a Pandora's box which everyone wishes to remain closed), and establishing a formal transit corridor through Lithuania, and more in terms of regional co-operation whereby the area's facilities can be used to generate trade and economic development for the benefit of all states in the area.

However, Western persuasion alone will not achieve such a sea-change; while there is a recognition among many of the actors that the excesses of the past have to be forgiven, even if they are not forgotten, and constructive co-operation emphasised, there is little doubt that this will *not* occur until the troops issue has been solved. "In the final analysis Russian armed force must leave Baltic territory ... that is accepted by all. However, the question of 'when and how' must be the subject of civilised negotiation conducted on the basis of mutual understanding and respect for the human rights of all involved ... There is no room in the Baltic nations for second class citizens or for outsiders in the democratic process ... We are dealing with one of the tragic consequences of the Cold War and the break up of the former Soviet Union. The welfare and the rights of individual citizens is at stake ... human rights like security is indivisable and no-one has a monopoly on the moral high ground in this respect. Failure to see the unique elements of this situation and to allow for them will have serious consequences for European security."[22]

These problems must be resolved if efforts to rebuild the economies of the Baltic Republics are to be successful. Only with political stability, democracy and respect for human rights will investment from the West be forthcoming. The key Western economic actor, certainly in the near term, will be the European Community which has made clear that its support for economic reconstruction is conditional upon positive developments at the political and social level.

5 The European Community Role

The European Community is a pillar of stability, security and economic dynamism with a key role to play during the post-Cold War transition in Europe. Its economic strengths and the size of its markets are such that non-members are seeking to join at an early date, or at least to secure affiliation or association leading eventually to full membership. The agreements forged during the December 1991 Maastricht Summit appeared to reinforce the Community's central role in European politics. European Monetary Union (EMU) and European Political Union (EPU) represented the culmination of a process of deepening which appeared to secure the future of a European union with a unified internal market and currency, and considerably strengthened political structures. However, foreign and security policies are still to be handled inter-governmentally, and the overall approach on defence remains cautious. The Maastricht text states only that the EC is: "to assert its identity on the international scene, in particular through the implementation of a common foreign and

[22] 'Summary of Conclusions: Stability and Security in the Baltic Region – Problems and Prospects', the Rose-Roth Seminar organised by the North Atlantic Assembly in conjunction with the Republic of Latvia Supreme Council, 27–29 April, 1992, Riga, Latvia.

security policy including the eventual framing of a common defence policy, which might in time lead to a common defence".

The text fails to reflect the view of Commission President Jacques Delors that "a common defence policy will be meaningless unless it reflects two types of solidarity: unity of analysis and action in foreign policy, and a reciprocal commitment to come to the aid of any member state whose integrity is threatened":[23] While the nine EC members of the WEU appear to be moving towards such commitments, they envisage a continuing WEU linkage with NATO. Indeed, even limited moves towards collective foreign policy, among other factors, prompt such unease in the Danish electorate that they rejected the Maastricht Treaty for European Union. This in turn has prompted a tide of Euro-scepticism in Scandinavia: "Two polls published by the evening papers *Expressen* and *Aftonbladet* in Stockholm suggested that of those questioned, 68 per cent and 45 per cent respectively were opposed to the entry of Sweden into the Community. Of those questioned, 32 per cent and 28 per cent wanted Sweden to join. In April, a poll by *Aftonbladet* had suggested that 37 per cent were in favour, 37 against and 25 per cent were undecided'. Similarly, in Norway 'an opinion poll published ... by the *Aftenposten* daily newspaper suggested that 53 per cent of Norwegians were opposed to the entry of Norway into the Community compared to 33 per cent who were in favour. A poll carried out by the newspaper three weeks ago suggested that 47 per cent were 'against' Europe and 39 per cent in favour".[24]

However, this adverse popular reaction appears to be a largely Western European phenomenon. The attraction of the Community in Eastern Europe remains undimmed, even if the prospect of membership remains long-term, and the urgent priorities are to secure economic assistance and access to the Community's market.

---

[23] Jacques Delors, The Alistair Buchan Memorial Lecture, London, 7 March 1991.
[24] 'Case Against EC Bolstered in Scandinavia', *The Times,* Friday, 5 June, 1992.

Economic Reconstruction in the East

The European Community will by no means be a panacea for East European economic problems, but it is able to offer significant support for local efforts to develop effective market economies. For example, it has acted swiftly in the Baltic Republics to support the evolution of a common market among the three countries and the removal of trade barriers. Consultations have been conducted about establishing their own currencies, and about economic specialisation. Since January 1992 Baltic countries have been included in the Community system of Generalised Preferences, and they are elegible for the G24 programme of economic aid which is being administered by the EC Commission. In March 1992 'first generation' affiliation agreements were signed removing quantitative restrictions on imports to the EC, reciprocal Most Favoured Nation (MFN) status; dialogue is continuing to establish so-called 'second generation' affiliation agreements, similar to those signed with Poland, Czechoslovakia and Hungary, which include a commitment to eventual EC membership. Considerable amounts of food and humanitarian aid are to be made available; 78 per cent of all aid to the CIS comes from EC sources.

Polish links with the Community are even more firmly established following successful negotiation of an association agreement. The Polish Government's long-term aim is EC membership, and it is prepared to accept the foreign security and defence policies elaborated through the WEU and EC; some Polish observers suggest that the country should be offered associate membership of the WEU. While there has been some adverse reaction to so-called 'foreign interference' in Poland's affairs, Polish policy remains supportive of close links with the EC. Whether and when this will include full membership of the Community is dependent upon the country's ability to meet EC requirements, both economic and political, and upon Community decisions on how best to widen membership.

EC Widening in the North

A range of suggestions exists on how best to widen the Community.

These include: the rapid inclusion of the rich EFTA countries, taking applications in turn chronologically, and dealing with applications in a series of 'waves': first the EFTA countries; then Czechoslovakia, Hungary and Poland; and finally the Baltic countries and Mediterranean applicants. It is widely acknowledged that EFTA countries pose few problems for the Community though they may have political reservations about membership. In contrast, the countries of the East have few political reservations about joining but will have great difficulty in meeting the economic requirements. The membership of the Ukraine and Russia is an outstanding issue; while many consider that Ukrainian membership is a possibility in the long-term, inclusion of Russia is widely felt to be impossible given the size of the country. Alternative suggestions include building a CIS economic community closely linked with the EC.

If the EMU is established under the Maastricht Treaty by 2000, East European countries will probably not be able to join until some years later. One short term possibility is to offer these countries 'affiliate' membership; an option rejected in the past as involving a second class status which would enable full *political* membership while not requiring full participation in all aspects of the Community's *economic* policy. EMU would thus be one of a number of policies to be adopted later.

While the outcome of EC deliberations on widening remains unclear, the attitudes of potential and actual applicants for membership are being clarified. The effects of the Danish vote remain to be clarified, but the Swedish and Finnish applications remain on the table and the Norwegian debate about possible membership is very much alive. The eventual decisions of these countries will certainly be affected by Denmark's future relations with the EC following the recent referendum result against the Maastricht Treaty; Danish withdrawal or ejection from the EC would have severe implications and perhaps strengthen the influence of those calling for a specifically 'Norden' grouping outside the Community.

An alternative would be the development of a two-tier or two-speed Community in which a core group of six or seven countries implemented the Maastricht provisions in full, while a second group 'dined à la carte', for example, remaining outside the EMU system or declining to participate in joint foreign, security and defence policies. Not surprisingly few Swedish or Finnish spokesmen are prepared to be drawn on these issues, contenting themselves with observing that they will meet existing Community requirements on acceding to the Treaty of Rome, and consider other Community decisions as and when these are taken. Notwithstanding the current ambiguities and disarray following the Danish vote, tempered somewhat by the subsequent positive decision of the Irish referendum, the applications of Nordic countries have generated considerable domestic concern about future security arrangements.

There is little doubt that Sweden will seek to continue its policy of maintaining non-alignment in peace-time in order to remain neutral during war. This policy has not precluded co-operation with others on foreign policy issues, for example, via the Nordic Council and the CSCE. In addition, Sweden has maintained a considerable national defence capability. But neutrality has been a dominant consideration, resulting for example in rejection of EC membership in the 1950s when neutrality in the Cold War was a priority. Following the changes in the international environment Sweden remains non-aligned but 'neutrality' no longer describes accurately the role it anticipates playing in the international community.

Thus Sweden is actively promoting the development of a new European security structure for which the CSCE provides a basis. It remains to be seen whether Swedish policy will be successful in taking the CSCE in this direction. More importantly in the near term the end of the Cold War means that EC membership is now possible. The economic benefits are widely understood. The European Economic Area was a first step to secure economic benefits, but the Swedish Government has decided that full membership is necessary to ensure that Sweden participates in the Community's decision-making. The rather loose provisions of the Maastricht Treaty on common foreign and security policy are felt to be compatible with Swedish security goals: it is prepared to participate in EC common foreign and security policy provided that such policy is based upon consensus. Participation in defence co-operation in particular must not be forced. For example, while Sweden appears prepared to co-operate in peace-keeping operations, whether organised by the UN, WEU, CSCE or EC, this has to remain a national decision. Future negotiations on membership will indicate whether this interpretation is accepted by the European Community.

The reasons for the Finnish decision to apply for EC membership broadly parallel those of the Swedish Government: economic advantage, access to markets, the four freedoms, co-operation on environmental issues, science and technology. Similarly, neutrality is less of a problem given the end of the Soviet threat, anticipated Russian troop reductions and a more benign Eastern neighbour. Many note that Finland has a window of opportunity to establish itself firmly in the West through EC membership. Postponement of a decision on entry might leave Finland alongside a group of non-member countries experiencing chronic economic, political and social problems.

Clearly, concerns exist about the future nature of the Community and these are shared by other EFTA applicants: the degree to which decisions are to be removed from domestic political process in the member states, how far subsidiarity will be applied and how effectively, the democratic deficit in the Community and the respective roles to be played by national member parliaments and the European Parliament. These are all questions for the future and do not seem likely to prevent continued efforts to join the Community. In this context security has two meanings: a) Finland will be a member of a Community which can encourage Russia to co-operate with its neighbours because of its need for EC aid and trade to develop its economy; and b) the Community may furnish a common defence force which can be deployed to help Finland in the event of a crisis. In the short-term most Finns stress economic and social advantages, defining security rather broadly in terms of trade, co-operation versus terrorism, and dealing with natural disasters, for example. The Government is fully aware that the Community may develop a common foreign and security policy and is prepared to apply for membership without reservation or qualification on this issue. Nevertheless, there is a continued underlying commitment to the effective national provision for adequate security and defence, reflected in the maintenance rather than reduction in levels of defence spending.

The stress on national self-reliance in security matters appears also to be growing in Norway, a staunch NATO member and the only one with a common border with Russia. However, the end of the Cold War has generated fears among some Norwegian observers that Norway will be marginalised as interest in 'the Russian problem' declines in an era of goodwill and co-operation. Some observers stress the continued need for security planning and adequate defence arrangements. They point out that war is not totally impossible and that negative changes in Russia could bring heightened tension. Therefore, adequate deterrence is still required which Norway can not provide alone; allies and rapid reinforcements continue to be needed and adequate arrangements for such support may decline if tensions remain low for considerable periods.

EC membership would help to counter this trend; the Community would not take kindly to military intervention against the territory of a member state. The evolution of a common EC foreign and security policy, and the strengthening of WEU, would reinforce the EC's role. Even in peace-time EC membership is likely to be helpful in case of differences between Norway and Russia. EC support could be useful in persuading a Russian government to compromise and enter into genuine negotiations. Observers also point out that Norwegian membership of the Community would contribute to the security of Europe, by assisting in the building of links with the East and preventing any re-nationalisation of defence policy. If the EC is to play the key role in preserving European peace and security in the future, Norway has to play its part.

Clearly, other factors in Norway run counter to this theme: objections of nationalists, on ideological grounds, and of particular interest groups, not least the farmers, may yet defeat attempts to join the Community. Indeed, reservations about the EC appear to be multiplying following the Danish referendum; how these political processes develop will influence strongly not only the EC's role in Europe but also the roles to be played by other 'security' institutions in the region. The fluidity which followed the collapse of communism in the East is now being mirrored in the West; the adage that the East is disintegrating and the West integrating is being called into question. Confusion, if not chaos, has to be avoided and steps taken to ensure that a stable European security environment is established, and the various actors in the Baltic system have to contribute to this process.

6 Conclusions

The end of the Cold War has promoted conscious efforts to redefine international 'security', reducing emphasis on military aspects and defence and stressing the importance of economic, political, social and environmental factors. The removal of the threat of direct Soviet invasion, the heavy investment of Western governments in the GATT negotiations and the Maastricht process, and the recognition by all of the need for economic reconstruction in the former Soviet empire have refocused decision-makers' attentions. *European* security is also increasingly considered as a whole rather than regionally or in an East-West context.

This sea-change in European thinking involves taking up ideas and concerns long central to 'Nordic' security views. This is facilitating the full participation in European security affairs of the Nordic countries which had sought to isolate themselves, in varying degrees, from the European mainstream: thus, Finland, Sweden and probably Norway will join the European Community in the decade ahead. As a further consequence the Nordic countries are all actively involved in efforts to build pan-European security structures via CSCE and the Baltic Council, for example. The traditional neutrals, Sweden and Finland, now appear to be prepared to abandon many aspects of their neutrality.

However, traditions have not been totally abandoned regarding national defence; Norway and Denmark remain committed to NATO. Finland and Sweden, notwithstanding applications to join the EC, have stressed their determination to retain *national* control over defence and security policy, albeit in co-operation with the CSCE and the Community in the future.

For the new states of Eastern Europe, economic reconstruction, entry into the world economic system and securing Western assistance are priorities. The EC is perceived as playing a key role; EC affiliation is at the top of most agendas. Unfortunately, Western reaction has been cautious, partly explained by doubts about the ability of local economies effectively to absorb Western aid. Indeed, concern about ethnic and social unrest, and increasingly realised fears about the likelihood of localised warfare, are reinforcing Western doubts. Frictions between the new governments of the Baltic States and local Russian military commanders cause particular concern in the Baltic region.

The response of the 'West' is two-fold: a) to retain significant defensive capability, either nationally or through NATO, b) to build and reinforce political contact with the new states of Eastern Europe and link this process with economic assistance. In a Europe of overlapping institutions a clear pattern has failed to emerge, but at least in the interim period of change, European security, whether broadly or narrowly defined, will be dominated by NATO in the West, Russia in the East, and an expanded but as yet undefined European Community. The area of greatest uncertainty lies in the middle, in the region stretching from the Baltic States in the North to the Black Sea in the South. As NATO membership is not offered and any collective defence arrangement with Russia is unacceptable the EC appears likely to play the key role. It is increasingly clear that the Community must offer at least close political linkage as a means of binding the newly independent states into the Western system; this of itself would do much to increase stability and security in the region. Full membership is a longer term prospect, but access to the Community's market for East European exports is essential in the meantime. Thus, the process of EC widening to the East should begin as quickly as possible in order to facilitate economic reconstruction and political stability. It should not be forgotten that the prospect of membership for Spain and Portugal was held out with these very aims in mind.

The Baltic littoral states have a key role to play in this process. Germany's traditional ties with Poland and the Baltic States and the success of its reconstruction programme in eastern Germany will crucially affect the overall stability of the region. The Nordic countries are already particularly active in Estonia, Latvia and Lithuania. In addition, their long-term commitment to the CSCE process, their experience in bridge-building, and past emphasis on non-military aspects of security constitute a body of experience which must be brought into play. But the rich countries of the region cannot alone meet the needs of their eastern neighbours; a broader Western effort, perhaps co-ordinated by the EC, is needed. Thus, Nordic participation in the European mainstream is essential; the 'Norden' option is indeed an echo from the past. The West has to act together to avert the dangers of chaos and violence in the East through a process of co-operative inter-action. This need not mean any 'grand design' of European union from the Atlantic to the Urals. Many of the problems have been identified and speedy action and practical assistance is required. Throughout the Cold War the Nordic countries developed a reputation for just this kind of effort which can now be directed to helping to establish a stable European security environment.

List of Participants

AALBU, Torbjörn: Norwegian Ambassador to Lavtia
AHRENS, Hans-Jürgen: Ministry of Labour, Schleswig-Holstein, Kiel
ALBREKTSEN, Knud-Erik: NATO Defence College, Rome
ARCHER, Clive: Centre for Defence Studies, Aberdeen
BRUHNS, Uwe: Federal Ministry of Defence, Bonn
DENTON, Geoffrey, Director, Wilton Park
ENGBERG, Katarina: International Institute for Strategic Studies, London

GOTTLIEB, Henning: The Danish Commission on Security and Disarmament, Copenhagen
GRANSTEDT, Pär: Member of Parliament and Member of Advisory Council on Foreign Affairs, Stockholm
HUGHES, Aneurin Rhys: Head, Office of the European Communities, Oslo
HULDT, Bo: Swedish Institute of International Affairs, Stockholm
ILONIEMI, Jaakko: Centre for Finnish Business and Policy Studies, Helsinki
INSERRA, Fabrizio: Ministry of Foreign Affairs, Rome
ISAKOVA, Irina: Institute of the USA and Canada, Moscow
JAKUBOWSKI, Krzysztof: Embassy of the Republic of Poland, London
KIVIMÄKI, Erkki: Ministry of Foreign Affairs, Helsinki
KIVINEN, Pentti: Centre for Finnish Business and Policy Studies, Helsinki
KLUMBYS, Egidijus: Supreme Council of the Republic of Lithuania, Vilnius
KNUDSEN, Bård Bredrup: Ministry of Defence, Oslo
KRISTOVSKIS, Girts: Supreme Council of the Republic of Latvia, Riga
KUDLINSKI, Romauld: University of Warsaw
LATTER, Richard: Wilton Park
LINDSTRÖM, Guy: Finnish Delegation to the Nordic Council
LOFTAAS, Arthur: Defence Command Headquarters, Oslo
LUCAS, Hans-Dieter: Federal Ministry of Foreign Affairs, Bonn
LYNE, Richard: Foreign and Commonwealth Office, London
MOSELEY, Christopher: BBC Monitoring, Caversham Park
NIKITIN, Alexander: Centre for Political and International Studies, Moscow
OLIPHANT, Craig: Royal Military Academy, Sandhurst
OLSEN, Jan: Defence Command Headquarters, Oslo
PARENTE, Gonzalo: Spanish Institute of Strategic Studies, Madrid
PUID i SCOTINI, Pau: Department for Foreign Initiatives, Barcelona
RAIG, Ivar: Supreme Council of the Republic of Estonia, Tallinn
RASMUSSEN, Peter: Ministry of Foreign Affairs, Copenhagen
SAARNILAHTI, Hannu: Finnish War College, Helsinki

SEEBODE, Christian: Federal Ministry of Foreign Affairs, Bonn

SHKUNDIN, Mark: Institute of World Economy and International Relations, Moscow

SKOGAN, John Kristen: Norwegian Institute of International Affairs, Oslo

SKRIVER, Ejgil: Danish Defence Headquarters, Vedbaek

STEFANOVICZ, Janusz: Institute of Political Studies, Warsaw

von STUDNITZ, Ernst-Jörg: Federal Ministry of Foreign Affairs, Bonn

TUCKER, Christopher: National Defence Headquarters, Ottawa

VAAHTORANTA, Tapani: Finnish Institute of International Affairs, Helsinki

Printed in the United Kingdom for HMSO
Dd294502 8/92 C6 G3397 10170